LLC

The Ultimate Guide to Starting a Limited Liability Company, and How to Deal with LLC Accounting and LLC Taxes

Contents

Introduction

A limited liability company (LLC) can be the right choice for any business owner seeking to reduce liability and protect his or her assets. This type of entity has several advantages over operating a sole proprietorship or partnership. Unlike a sole proprietorship or partnership, an LLC shields the owner or owners from liability, and unlike a more complex corporation, management structure is loose, there is no board of directors to answer to, and with an LLC being a pass-through organization, no double taxation which corporations are subject to unless one elects to be taxed as a C or S corporation. So, let's explore the ins and outs of an LLC and see if it's right for you.

Chapter 1 – LLC's Explained, Pros, Cons

There are several types of business entities a new business owner may consider when starting out, and it is important for an entrepreneur understand each type of entity and which is most appropriate for his/her situation, the simplest form being a sole proprietorship or partnership. In a sole proprietorship one is in business for him or herself, although many finance activities are kept separate from the owner's personal finance activities. A partnership is similar to a sole proprietorship, but there are at least two or more parties involved, and in some cases, the parties may have to file a certificate of partnership with the state they are doing business. The next evolution and focus of this book is the limited liability company, or LLC. We'll discuss this more in detail in the following chapters. Finally, at the top of the hierarchy are the various forms of corporations. Corporations are a legal entity, operated under state law, and are restricted by its charter. Small business corporations, or S-corporations, are much like an LLC, but must meet strict IRS guidelines, and in return, avoid double-taxation much like regular corporations.

Types of Business Liability

Premises liability- If you own a physical space open to the general public or even limited to select clients, you may want to invest in premises liability coverage. Accidents can happen on your property - from a customer's simple slip and fall to your own employee doing something negligent, resulting in injury.

Operations liability- If you own a service business and operate from your central place of business, such as a building contractor, such a policy will cover liabilities covered while away from headquarters.

Product Liability- If you make a product for consumption, you face a certain degree of risk. The more complex the product, the risk goes up considerably. For example, an automobile has numerous risks as compared to a hammer, which can be dangerous but has far less moving parts.

Completed operation liability- Finished work also has risk (we'll cover more on that later).

Employment practices liability- If you have employees, you face this risk. This comes in the form of breach of contract, discrimination, sexual harassment, and wrongful termination. You can minimize this risk with an employment practices liability insurance policy.

Errors and omissions liability- Service businesses are particularly vulnerable to this type of liability. A doctor can be sued for malpractice, and even an or consultant accountant can give incorrect advice. Errors and omissions liability insurance can help minimize risk in this area.

Cyber liability- As businesses increasingly store data in the cloud or in databases, while storing a name and address can be a small concern, when the degree includes more sensitive data such as banking and credit card info, social security numbers, and health information, the risk of hacking goes up. A cyber liability can help a business owner recover from this type of risk and interruption.

Liquor or intoxication liability- This type of liability applies to restaurants and bars, or anywhere alcohol is served. It also applies to venues where perhaps patrons furnish their own alcohol. For example, if your business is hosting a wedding reception, you also face risk. Check with your insurance agent to ensure you are covered for liquor liability.

Different Types of Business Entities

Sole Proprietorship- Single-owner business, he or she has unlimited liability for business debts, income and losses reported on his/her personal tax filing

Unlimited Partnership- Two or more owners are exposed to unlimited liability for business debts. His or her portion of income or loss is reported on a separate section of their personal income tax filing.

Limited Partnership- Similar to unlimited partnership for tax purposes, although debt exposure is only limited to each owner's individual contribution to the partnership.

Corporation- Limited liability for investors, creditors may only sue against the assets of the corporation, double taxed as the corporation pays taxes on its income and dividends are also taxed for each investor.

"C" Corporation- Form of business where liability is limited, but profits are passed to the owners and taxed at the individual level.

"S" Corporation- Hybrid form of business which is treated like a partnership for tax purposes and a corporation for other purposes.

Limited Liability Company- See below

A limited liability company (LLC) is a type of business entity. It is unique in that it combines elements of a sole proprietorship or partnership with elements of a corporation. As the name implies, the limited liability portion shields its owner or partners from liability much like a corporation, but, like a sole proprietorship or partnership, it is taxed in a similar fashion. There are many advantages to this type of business structure, as well as some cautions any person considering this type of entity should be aware of.

The advantages to forming an LLC include the ability to shield the owner or partners or members from liability of both acts and debts. Not every type of company would need this type of protection though. For instance, a freelance painter with an Etsy shop faces very little personal risk if a customer is not happy with a painting purchased online; on the other hand, a souvenir shop owner faces a potentially huge liability should a customer get injured slipping on a wet floor or a supplier demands payment for a pile of invoices, but not necessarily from a defective keychain purchased at the shop. Another example where an LLC makes sense is for a real estate investment property owner or landlord. Ideally, each property should have its own LLC established. This can limit risk exposure to that single property, and it becomes even more important as the property owner acquires more property, or to even shield the landlord's personal home from liability. This applies to all business owners as he or she becomes more successful and acquires more assets. It is important to shield these assets from a costly lawsuit. Additional protection can be covered by insurance or an umbrella policy, but personal assets have an extra layer of protection because the LLC is treated as a separate entity and if your business is being sued, your home and family may be shielded from additional damages as well.

Recent case law shows how a single member LLC can offer limited protections in a claim against the LLC and the owner/member. In the case of Strum & Strum v. Harb Development, LLC, the Strums alleged that John Harb built a house that lacked an adequate concrete slab, and the first and second floors deviated from construction plans. Harb filed a motion to strike all motions against him in an individual capacity claiming the Strums had insufficient evidence to warrant piercing the corporate veil. The Strums appealed, and the outcome of the lawsuit was had Harb been found negligent or was guilty of fraud, the court would have ruled in the Strum's favor and he would have been held personally liable for his actions. In this case, the veil was pierced under the term known as alter ego liability, where Harb was so closely connected to his company it was hard to tell Harb and his company apart.

There are other exceptions which may not shield members of an LLC from liability, and they vary by state. A charging order is when a legal order is issued to the LLC in which a member's profits may be required to pay off a debt. Foreclosure on LLC interest is where a company may foreclose on a member's interest in order to satisfy a personal debt. Order of dissolution is where the company is closed down and income from the sale of assets are used to pay off a debt to a creditor.

Taxes are also much more simplified for an LLC compared to a traditional corporation. They are treated much the same as a sole-proprietorship or partnership and are passed through to the owner or members. This concept is known as pass-through taxation. In the case of a single-member LLC, as in the case of a sole proprietorship, tax for the business is reported and calculated on Schedule C of an income tax return. For a partnership, business income is reported and calculated on Form 1065.

Another advantage of an LLC is they are more resistant to "fire sale" investors. A fire sale is where the business is facing bankruptcy and is selling off assets. In the case of a corporation, if shares are sold in a stock exchange, those shares may be available for highly-discounted prices, which also puts a corporation at risk of a takeover bid.

Perhaps the biggest advantage to an LLC is that it's relatively easy to set up as compared to an S or C-corporation or corporation, and still offers many of the benefits of a sole proprietorship or partnership in how the business is run.

The disadvantages of an LLC should also be mentioned. For one, there are additional steps compared to starting a sole proprietorship or partnership. A single member LLC may also not receive all the liability protections a multi-member LLC affords, this is something that can be avoided by giving another member or a long-time employee a minor stake in the business (like 2-5%). Another downside, being much like a sole proprietorship or partnership, if someone wants to leave the company, as part of the operating agreement, the company may dissolve (check your state laws). This can be avoided and covered in the operating agreement (which will be discussed later), as long as the business fulfills its obligations, a departing member may allow his or her equity to be satisfied either by immediate payment or some other type of compensation arrangement. Another disadvantage is additional costs. There are additional filing fees which are usually paid annually. Banking is also handled differently compared to a sole proprietorship or partnership. Checks cannot be simply cashed if paid directly to an owner or partner for business purposes, these checks must be cashed through a corporate bank account, which also adds costs. Since an LLC and owner are separate, an owner is subject to additional personal taxes, such as unemployment taxes, which a member of a partnership or sole proprietorship would not be subject to. One final big caution is each owner/partner must keep personal assets and transactions separate from the LLC's activities. Once these elements are comingled, this is when piercing the corporate veil occurs. Piercing the corporate veil is a legal term where a court may have found that once personal and business transactions are intermingled, it may be difficult to distinguish these transaction types. For instance, if a business credit card is used for one's personal expenses, a limited liability status may be ignored. Logically, if this happens and the LLC is sued, the company's assets may be at risk along with a member's personal assets. We will discuss more examples in the following chapter.

It is important in a multi-member LLC that decision-making is carefully outlined as to how voting is handled in a stalemate and when meetings occur detailed notes should be taken. For instance, if there are four members in a member-managed company, all owners have an equal stake in a construction company. Three of the four managers object to taking on a new bridge construction project, the fourth manager is enthusiastic about the new undertaking, but since he was outvoted, the company will move on or focus on to existing projects. Now consider that fourth member has a 50% ownership in the firm. This is where outlining decision-making can help avoid conflict. With a firm outline, perhaps the majority stakeholder gets to guide the company's direction, but without this process documented this could lead to disagreements and a potential lawsuit. Another complex matter would be a manager-managed LLC. Perhaps the managers want to take on a risky, but profitable project, but the actual members are in disagreement. This is where outlining how these situations are handled can help avoid confusion and frustration.

Chapter 2 – LLC Case Law: A Cautionary Tale

Limited liability also covers you up to an extent, but not all conduct by members is protected nor right in the eyes of the court. This chapter explains actual cases and provides real-life examples of where business owners went awry. You can skip over this chapter if true crime or courthouse drama isn't your cup of tea, but it would be wise for any business owner or manager to understand how these circumstances arise and how to avoid them in the first place.

In DeWitt Truck Brokers v. W. Ray Flemming Fruit Co., Flemming acted as the middleman between the farmers and fruit purchasers. Flemming paid DeWitt Truck Brokers to transport fruit, which Flemming personally guaranteed he'd pay them back even if his corporation couldn't. Flemming was unable to pay Dewitt back on time and they sued Flemming personally. Flemming argued he wasn't liable and that the corporation was responsible for the debt. The district court ruled in favor of DeWitt Truck Brokers and Flemming appealed. Ultimately, the court upheld the original judgment and Flemming was personally liable for the debt. A word of caution is for managers to be cautious of providing a personal social security number for a corporate credit card. This may be necessary for a fledgling company, but this in many cases is similar to the Flemming case, where your social security number is just like personally guaranteeing that the credit card will be paid every month, otherwise the creditor may go after the manager.

While a two-member LLC can streamline decision making, it can also cause difficulties. In Cline v. Grelock, Jeremy Cline and Ryan Grelock opened a recovery and towing business. Cline was required to contribute $25,000 as part of the operating agreement, their relationship quickly deteriorated. Grelock shut down the LLC and eventually opened a separate LLC with his wife and brought along a vehicle used in the Cline and Grelock venture in which Cline guaranteed a loan for. Cline sued Grelock, but all parties' motions were rejected. The court did find that Cline was entitled to remedies for Grelock's breaches and dissolution of their prior business, however they were unable to determine how to properly compensate Cline. Ultimately, Grelock was stuck with all litigation costs.

In a single-member LLC, it is important to cover for worst-case scenarios in an operating agreement. In the case of Player Wire Wheels, Ltd, the single member had passed away. The member had pledged his membership interest to his ex-wife. The estate had failed to pay a debt and the challenge was whether or not the ex-wife had the authority to file bankruptcy on behalf of the LLC. Being the executor of the estate, the court did eventually find that the ex-wife did have authority to do so. A simple amendment to the operating agreement could have probably eliminated this from being an issue.

Your LLC agreement may also be grounds for legal action. In Kelly v. Blum, the plaintiff, Thomas Kelly, President of Marconi Broadcasting Company, LLC brought suit against Blum, a manager of Marconi Broadcasting Company, LLC after a proposed merger. During the course of business, Marconi was formed to acquire broadcast rights and licenses, and from 2006-2007 entered into various finance agreements to purchase a broadcast tower and FCC license due to lack of revenues. Upon securing an additional loan and security agreement, and as part of this, he executed an amended LLC agreement in which the lender MBC Lender, LLC, held Class

A membership units, Kelly held Class B units, and MBC Lender also held Class C units. In 2008, a board of Managers meeting was held and the Class A and Class C managers (of which included Blum) voted to terminate Kelly as President of Marconi. The court did rule that proper notice was given to Kelly as set forth in the amended operating agreement, but Kelly did have a suit against the defendants for breach of fiduciary duties of loyalty and for entering into a self-interested merger. Blum was also found guilty of defaming Kelly relating to his alleged incompetence and lack of ability to run Marconi.

As you will learn, many states don't even require an operating agreement. In the Kansas case of Winning Streak, Inc. v. Winning Streak Sports, LLC a court of appeals ruled in favor of the defendant. The plaintiff, an individual member, claimed he had a 49% stake in a business. The lack of an operating agreement led the court to conclude that the individual only had a .96% stake in the business. A properly executed operating agreement outlining membership stakes and payout amounts would have alleviated this problem.

Greed can also get in the way of operations running smoothly. In Moede v. Pochter, an LLC member sued the other members for breach of contract. The plaintiff made a demand that money be paid out to him and certain other members prior to other members. This demand was also made by a lawyer, and the court found that this demand was in his own self-interest and that it was unacceptable. The operating agreement superseded statute and found it would breach fiduciary duty if one member were to get preferential distribution over another member.

Dissolution is also important and should be executed properly, otherwise settling debts can be a huge problem. In Resort Point Custom Homes, LLC v. Tait, the Delaware LLC and construction business was dissolved due to disputes among its members. The dissolution resulted in two new LLC's forming. Tait provided plumbing services for the original LLC. Projects were then divided between the new LLC's and as such one of them set to collect amounts owed by Tait. Tait denied he owed anything to the new LLC and sought to offset that amount by an amount owed to him on another project from the original LLC. The court ruled that part of the dissolution process for the original LLC was to pay all claims and obligations and the assets be distributed to all creditors and members. The court found that the new LLC were neither creditors nor members and the only provision made for Tait's claim was a letter directing him to send bills to the new LLC, of which he had no contractual obligation. Ultimately the new LLC had the burden of proof, claiming that it had contractual rights to the projects and their claimed amounts.

It is important for all members to understand obligations of being part of an LLC, to act in a responsible manner, and to observe all contractual obligations whether between two parties or to understand duties as part of an LLC articles of organization. Many of the above cases could have been avoided had the individuals affected discussed potential outcomes, weighed the alternatives, and behaved in a prudent and rational manner.

Source:
https://www.baylor.edu/content/services/document.php/140022.pdf

Chapter 3 – LLC and Piercing the Corporate Veil

Piercing the corporate veil and duties of a member deserves its own chapter. It is both a cautionary measure and one every LLC or corporation should understand and avoid. Members should also understand their primary fiduciary duties. There are no good reasons to go through all the extra measures and expense of filing and starting an LLC if you are not making sure to avoid exposing yourself to personal liability and not doing what's right for your LLC. Here are some mistakes that have been well documented in case law and how some member or managers got into hot water and how you can avoid it.

Fraud, injustice, or wrongdoing to a third party is an easy way to find yourself named in a lawsuit. This applies to any business, but with an LLC you also put your personal assets at risk. As mentioned in the previous chapter, even a multi-member LLC can find perhaps one partner putting his or her equity stake at risk if found guilty of fraud or wrongdoing. In a single-member LLC this can be even more perilous. Suppose a sole member was found guilty in a tort claim and suddenly started to transfer assets to his or her personal accounts, or even another company, to shield these funds in a judgment. Even though the fraud is not directly tied to the tort, it can put the member's personal assets at risk. Had the owner simply left the money as is, he could have preserved his personal wealth, or at least, the other company's assets.

Alter ego occurs when it's difficult to tell a corporation and individual apart. An example was already mentioned in the Harb case. How does one avoid this confusion? You could distance yourself further from your LLC by choosing another name other than your full birth name or the name on your driver's license if you really want to create a separate identity. Just food for thought.

Separate transactions should always be maintained. Once personal trips are comingled with a business trip, it is easy for a member to have his or her personal assets put at risk. When in doubt, use your personal credit or debit card instead of the company card for travel where little or no business is involved (checking your emails while on vacation does not constitute a business trip) to reduce risk, no matter how inconvenient it may be.

Maintaining adequate working capital is essential for a business to run smoothly. It can help you get through the slow times and allow strategic growth decisions when the time is right. When one has enough sales and inventory to cover upcoming expenses and payroll, it makes operations smooth and stress-free; when there are shortcomings, it is important to not dip into personal assets to cover expenses. It may be wise to even maintain your business account and personal checking accounts at separate banks to avoid the temptation of comingling funds. Understand your financials and you will be able to react swiftly by leveraging your business when proper.

The final caution: maintain corporate formalities. This is more of a problem with family-owned LLC's where a looser structure may be inherent with such a business. If you outline certain criteria in your articles of organization, be sure to follow them, no matter how mundane or formal, in spite of an otherwise lax company culture. This especially applies to annual filings and other ordinary filings such as taxes. If one is required to document activity, be sure to maintain these records and file them in a timely manner. It should also be noted that you should provide the world with corporate notice, for instance, if you enter into a contract, ensure that you are acting on behalf of your organization and not as an individual. If you sign a loan contract, be sure your company's full name is also included in signature lines (i.e. ABC Jelly, Inc.). Business cards, letterhead, etc. also should include the full name of your organization with "Inc." or "LLC" included. This applies to passing out business cards to clients or giving official notice to vendors or customers.

The fiduciary duties of a member include loyalty and care. Under the duty of loyalty, a member must put the success and benefits of the LLC above his or her own advantages. It would be in poor taste if Jack from ABC Jelly were to also be an investor in a small start-up jam company, and this may, in fact, be in violation of state law. The duty of care requires a member to act in good faith and exercise reasonable care in the directing of business activities of an LLC. An example would be Jill as part of ABC Jelly LLC buying a land for a new processing facility site unseen, and without researching the land history, only to discover the site was a former chemical manufacturing site and the land requires extensive clean-up to make it usable. Jill did not show care and did not act in good faith.

As you can see, piercing the corporate veil can be performed in several ways and the fiduciary duties of loyalty and care are important. If you avoid these common missteps, your LLC will not only run smoothly, your liability will be very limited, and, most importantly, your assets will be shielded from the actions performed by you or a member of your company.

Chapter 4 – Steps to Starting an LLC

As mentioned in Chapter 1, if you run a business where you face potential liabilities, often an LLC may be the ideal solution to protect what you've worked hard for and help protect your loved ones. Of course, there are steps to starting an LLC, but the process is fairly easy, and there only a few steps to make it happen. We'll cover those steps in detail in this chapter.

An LLC is a good idea for the conditions mentioned previously, but it is not something every business owner should immediately jump into. For instance, a start-up may have huge costs in the beginning to get established, and if the sales or income is not sufficient to cover the expense of an LLC, it might be smarter to delay filing. This is especially true if little is at risk; for instance, if a product is being in development stages and is being built by a contract vendor, or a similar situation with a concept not ready for market. Another reason to delay or avoid an LLC is simply determining if a huge liability exists. For instance, a freelance writer who creates non-fiction novels has very little liability compared to a general contractor. That's not to say the writer should be reckless, but if one exercises due diligence, liability can be reduced to almost zero, or a proper insurance policy might be sufficient to eliminate most or all risk. Finally, timing may be a consideration. It may be more advantageous to delay starting an LLC if you are near the end of a tax year. Filing late in the tax year may make your tax situation more work than delaying it for a month or so. If your situation favors a delay in starting an LLC, you may be able to reserve the name of your LLC. There is usually a fee for this, but if you have a unique product or concept, claiming a name can be a smart marketing move. As always, consult with a tax professional to see what works best for your situation.

Starting an LLC is straightforward and one most business owners are capable of handling on their own. First, one must choose a name. There are databases for searching business names that can determine if your name is unique. The name, of course, is critical and not only identifies your presence in the business community, but it also is something you can build a brand behind. It is also important to check if the URL is available if you choose to establish a web presence; this can help eliminate confusion, as you may find ABC Jelly would make a great business name, only to find ABCJelly.com is a registered URL and there may be costs to acquire it, or it may not even be an option. In today's increasingly technologically-reliant marketplace, a website may not only be a place to explain more about your business, but it can also be a place to establish additional sales, be a cheap source of marketing or gain you leads or fans.

One has to consider in which state they will form their LLC. If you have a physical location in your home state it may be required to form there, but if you have a consulting business or will be conducting business beyond your state's borders you may be able to register as a foreign LLC. While it may seem obvious that your home state may be the easiest choice, some states have streamlined the process, including online registration, and some may offer lower fees. You may have heard of a Delaware LLC and there is good reason. It is one of the most business-friendly jurisdictions in the

United States. Delaware does not tax out-of-state income, their fees are low, and they have a dedicated court, called Chancery Court, that deals exclusively with business matters. This can greatly reduce the time it takes to dispute and settle business concerns. Nevada is another pro-business jurisdiction. It shares traits with Delaware in that profits aren't taxed, they do not tax inheritances or capital gains, and there are also no franchise taxes. Nevada also is lax with other requirements, such as not requiring annual meetings. Another solid reason businesses incorporate in Nevada is the state does not share info with the Internal Revenue Service, so if you run a discrete business or simply enjoy a degree of privacy, this may be a great option. Wyoming is new to the LLC game but offers similar benefits to Nevada in that business income and franchises are not taxed. Another trait shared with Nevada is that tax information is not shared with the IRS. It's easy to see why many businesses choose to form an LLC in states other than their own.

Owner contribution or member contributions are also important to forming an LLC. An owner may put up the necessary cash to start the company, if there are partners one may contribute assets such as property to the venture. It is important that the fair market value of asset contributions be discussed and agreed upon to determine that member's stake in the business. Another consideration is to be sure to book the equity properly into your accounting system. We'll discuss more about accounting and taxes in the next chapter.

All states require you file an article of organization. This document creates the LLC in your state, which there is a filing fee which can be as little as $100 to as much as $800. If you need an expedited application, many states will accommodate such a request for an additional fee. This document outlines your business purpose, identifies your business location, length of existence, if not perpetual, such as an LLC that has been established around a patent, describes your operating structure, and most importantly, identifies your business as a legal entity in your state. A registered agent will also need to be established, and is the entity who accepts legal notices, and lawsuits, on behalf of your business. In some states, the secretary of state may be required to be the registered agent. Lastly, your managers and members of the LLC should be named.

Another step is to create an operating agreement, although not all states require this and it is not usually a concern when things are running smoothly. A written operating agreement can be executed by the business owner, or with the help of an attorney or agency. Some states may have a template which covers the basic information required to file and in the proper format. The basic info that must be included in your articles is: LLC name, the LLC's registered agent, the LLC's business address, effective date of your LLC, duration of your LLC, and if your LLC will be member or manager-managed. We should discuss duration; for instance, it would be easy to determine an absolute life of an LLC if is attached to an asset such as a residential property. If the property is sold, or, sadly, destroyed, the LLC would cease to exist. It is important if you have other partners involved to discuss in detail how day-to-day management is handled. You may hold a minor stake in a two-member LLC, but your partner doesn't want to be involved with daily management and may elect a more passive role. These should be discussed before documents are filed with the state. It can cover how ownership is divided, how voting rights are handled in a partnership, legal rights and responsibilities, how profits are distributed, how management is handled, if interest is paid for member contributions, and, as mentioned in Chapter 1, if a partner is to leave, outlines how that situation is handled. That may entail paying out the owner's share in a lump sum or via installments. It may also outline whether to replace the member or not. This is also where the member or members want to consider continuation of the business; if you feel this business may be of value long after members leave or retire, this is where buy-sell provisions may be added and should include a specific dollar amount in case of member fall-out. You may have concerns about growth, and, not to worry, states are flexible and allow you to amend an operating agreement, from increasing a buy-out amount to perhaps adding another member where contributions could be diluted. Many states will require additional fees when there is a change in management structure.

An announcement may also be necessary. There are three states that still require publishing a notice, and this usually entails a small fee paid to have your notice published in a local newspaper or publication. In some of the states that require publication they may also require an Affidavit of Publication be submitted with your file. The affidavit is proof by a notary public, or person authorized to administer an oath, attesting that the required publication for the specified terms took place. There will also be fees for these services as well. Do not ignore this step if you live in one of the three states that make this a requirement. According to New York state law, failing to make this announcement can allow the state to cease your operations until you have complied with this mandate.

The next step to consider is if you plan on doing business in other states. An LLC for a convenience store will have limited scope outside of its home state, unless, of course, the store expands to more than one location. An internet-based seller would do business not only in other states, but possibly in other countries. When doing business in other states, you may likely need to register to do business in those other states. It's a similar process to registering for your home state; in addition, you will need a registered agent for each state you plan on doing business.

The final step is to get all the required licenses and permits. If you are starting fresh or transitioning from a partnership or sole proprietorship you will need to register for a new Employee Identification Number (EIN) and this can be accomplished on the IRS website. Most cities or counties require a business license and there are annual fees associated with that. These are usually tied to your annual revenues. Your state might require a seller's permit to keep tabs of sales taxes. To top it off, certain industries may have additional filing requirements; for instance, a fuel retailer may have to file environmental permits or require testing before opening for business. A doctor or lawyer will need a license to practice in his or her own chosen state. Barbers and real estate agents may also have state certifications they must pass to begin work. A general contractor usually requires a contractor's license before beginning any type of work. A restaurant that wishes to serve alcohol may have to file for a permit or license to do so. Health permits may be required by local jurisdictions for food establishments, and a fire department may need to sign off before occupying a new retail or office space.

It's important to mention that once all has been filed with the appropriate agencies, not all is set in stone. Just like your business grows and needs change, you may need to file and update your articles of organization. This is where filing an amendment is necessary. An amendment may be required if you change your business name, relocate your headquarters, or add new members; as long as the amendment doesn't violate the provisions set forth by your state, an amendment will be required in most situations. As with most steps of formation, an amendment can be handled by a member or one may use a service to file.

An LLC may not be the end-all solution for all types of businesses. This applies to certain professions. Lawyers, accountants, and doctors may have individual practices and these professions require licenses, and with these types of professional service businesses an LLC does would not be appropriate. These types of businesses can file for a professional limited liability company/PLLC or a limited liability partnership or LLP depending on your state's requirements. In this type of business, one partner carries the liability for another or other partners in the business.

Another option is to consider that perhaps your business might already exceed the capabilities or limits of an LLC. In situations where you may have several investors interested in bringing your product or concept to market or your business to the next level, it may be best to form a corporation to make investing and offering an initial public offering (IPO) more feasible. Of course, having a public company also has its challenges, such as answering to shareholders, special accounting considerations, and strict oversight on financial reporting.

It should also be mentioned that there are service providers that can assist with filing an LLC. The extent of assistance can be very basic, from just acting as your agent for legal documentation, to others offering a full suite of services and charging accordingly for a breadth of services offered. These agencies can be valuable and save frustration but do your homework to make sure the service is legitimate, and research the satisfaction rate through the Better Business Bureau or consumer reviews on these service providers.

Chapter 5 – LLC State-Specific Guidelines

Here we discuss the specifics required for each state and list them in alphabetical order. Most states follow a same basic filing process as was outlined in the previous chapter and are as follows:

1. Name your LLC
2. Select a registered agent
3. File your articles of organization
4. Form an operating agreement
5. Obtain an EIN

In this chapter we explain more on annual reporting and any associated fees and if it is even required to file, as well as discuss foreign LLC filing procedures. Many states restrict naming conventions, such as including the words Attorney, Bank, or University in a business name, unless a licensed individual is part of the LLC. Others also restrict naming that might cause a business to be confused with a state or federal government agency such as FBI, Treasury, Secret Service, etc. We also discuss the nuances of each state, as some states may have additional steps to form or maintain your LLC.

Alabama

Domestic filing fee: $150

Renewal: $150

Foreign filing fee: $250

Expedited fee: $100

Entity name must include Limited Liability Company, Ltd. Liability Company, or and abbreviation thereof. Certificate of Name Reservation is required prior to filing formation documents. A certificate of formation operating is required to be filed with the probate judge or secretary of state, an operating agreement is not required but it is highly advisable to keep this on file with your registered agent. Foreign LLC's have a similar filing procedure.

Alaska

Domestic filing fee: $100

Renewal: $100

Foreign filing fee: $250

Entity name must contain "Limited Liability Company", or any abbreviation thereof. Standard filing procedure, with the exception of an initial report due within 6 months of organization. Both foreign and domestic LLC's then file a report every 2 years, due on January 2nd of the filing year.

Arizona

Domestic filing fee: $50

Renewal: $0

Foreign filing fee: $150

Entity name must contain "Limited Liability Company", or any abbreviation thereof. Standard filing procedure with no option for same or next day processing. No annual reporting required.

Arkansas

Domestic filing fee: $50

Foreign filing fee: $300

Entity name must contain "Limited Liability Company", or any abbreviation thereof. Standard filing procedure and usually can be completed within one to two business days. No annual reporting required.

California

Domestic filing fee: $70

Renewal: $800

Foreign filing fee: $70

Entity name must contain "Limited Liability Company", or any abbreviation thereof. Standard filing procedure, with exception of a Statement of Information report due within 90 days of organization. Both foreign and domestic LLC's must file a report every year.

Colorado

Domestic filing fee: $50

Renewal: $10

Foreign filing fee: $100

Entity name must contain "Limited Liability Company", or any abbreviation thereof including "Ltd.". Standard filing procedure, with exception of an operating agreement is not required to filed with the state, however it is highly recommended you do keep one on file if there is more than one member. Both foreign and domestic LLC's must file a report every year.

Connecticut

Domestic filing fee: $120

Renewal: $20

Foreign filing fee: $120

Entity name must contain "Limited Liability Company", or any abbreviation thereof. Standard filing procedure. Annual reporting required but no late fee if filed late, but the state may revoke a "good standing status;" LLC may be dissolved after 1 year for failure to file an annual report.

Delaware

Domestic filing fee: $90

Renewal: $300

Foreign filing fee: $200

Entity name must contain "Limited Liability Company", or any abbreviation thereof. Standard filing procedure. Annual reporting not required, but Alternative Entity Tax of $300 due June 1 of each year.

Florida

Domestic filing fee: $125

Renewal: $138.75

Foreign filing fee: $100

Entity name must contain "Limited Liability Company", or any abbreviation thereof. Standard filing procedure. Annual reporting must be filed electronically and received between January 1st and May 1st.

Georgia

Domestic filing fee: $100

Renewal: $50

Foreign filing fee: $225

Entity name must contain "Limited Liability Company", or any abbreviation thereof including "LC" and "Ltd.". Standard filing procedure. Annual reporting must be received between January 1st and April 1st.

Hawaii

Domestic filing fee: $50

Renewal: $15

Foreign filing fee: $50

Expedited fee: $25

Entity name must contain "Limited Liability Company", or any abbreviation thereof. Standard filing procedure. Both foreign and domestic LLC's must file a report every year due by the end of the quarter within the anniversary date in which the LLC was formed.

Idaho

Domestic filing fee: $100

Renewal: $0

Foreign filing fee: $100

Expedited fee: $20

Entity name must contain "Limited Liability Company", or any abbreviation thereof. Standard filing procedure. Both foreign and domestic LLC's must file a report every year due by June 30th.

Illinois

Domestic filing fee: $150

Renewal: $75, $300 if filed online

Foreign filing fee: $150

Entity name must contain "Limited Liability Company", or any abbreviation thereof. Standard filing procedure. Both foreign and domestic LLC's must file a report every year within 60 days of the anniversary date in which the LLC was formed.

Indiana

Domestic filing fee: $95 online, $100 by mail

Renewal: $50

Foreign filing fee: $90

Entity name must contain "Limited Liability Company", or any abbreviation thereof. Standard filing procedure. Operating not required but recommended especially for LLC's with multiple members. Both foreign and domestic LLC's then file a biennial report due by the end of the month of the anniversary date in which the LLC was formed.

Iowa

Domestic filing fee: $50

Renewal: $60

Foreign filing fee: $100

Entity name must contain "Limited Liability Company", or any abbreviation thereof. Standard filing procedure. Both foreign and domestic LLC's then file a biennial report due on April 1st of odd years.

Kansas

Domestic filing fee: $160 online, $165 by mail

Renewal: $50 online, $55 by mail

Foreign filing fee: $165

Entity name must contain "Limited Liability Company", or any abbreviation thereof. Standard filing procedure. Operating agreement not required but it's highly recommended to keep one on file. Annual reporting required and due by the 15th day of the fourth month after your company's tax closing month. For example, if you close taxes on December 31st, your annual report is due April 15th.

Kentucky

Domestic filing fee: $40

Renewal: $30 online, $15 by mail

Foreign filing fee: $90

Entity name must contain "Limited Liability Company", or any abbreviation thereof. Standard filing procedure. Operating agreement not required but it's highly recommended to keep one on file. Annual reporting required and due between January 1st and June 30th each year.

Louisiana

Domestic filing fee: $100

Renewal: $30 online, $15 by mail

Foreign filing fee: $90

Expedited fee: $30

Entity name must contain "Limited Liability Company", or any abbreviation thereof. Standard filing procedure. Operating agreement not required but it's highly recommended to keep one on file. Annual reporting required and due on or before the anniversary date which the LLC was formed.

Maine

Domestic filing fee: $175

Renewal: $85, $150 for foreign

Foreign filing fee: $250

Expedited fee: $50 for 24-hour service, $100 for immediate

Entity name must contain "Limited Liability Company", or any abbreviation thereof. Standard filing procedure, operating agreement not required, but highly recommended to maintain written file. Both foreign and domestic LLC's must file a report every year due by June 1st.

Maryland

Domestic filing fee: $100

Renewal: $300, counties may have additional fees

Foreign filing fee: $100

Expedited fee: $50

Entity name must contain "Limited Liability Company", or any abbreviation thereof. Standard filing procedure, operating agreement not required, but highly recommended to maintain a written file. Both foreign and domestic LLC's must file a report called the personal property return, due every year on April 15th.

Massachusetts

Domestic filing fee: $500

Renewal: $500

Foreign filing fee: $500

Entity name must contain "Limited Liability Company", or any abbreviation thereof. Standard filing procedure, operating agreement required and may be verbal or written, but highly recommended to maintain written file. Both foreign and domestic LLC's must file an annual report due by the anniversary date of when the LLC was formed.

Michigan

Domestic filing fee: $50

Renewal: $25

Foreign filing fee: $50

Entity name must contain "Limited Liability Company", or any abbreviation thereof. Standard filing procedure, operating agreement not required, but highly recommended to maintain a written file. Both foreign and domestic LLC's must file an annual report due February 15th.

Minnesota

Domestic filing fee: $135 by mail, $155 online or in person

Renewal: $0

Foreign filing fee: $185 by mail, $205 in person

Entity name must contain "Limited Liability Company", or any abbreviation thereof. Standard filing procedure, operating agreement not required, but highly recommended to maintain a written file. Both foreign and domestic LLC's must file an annual report due December 31st. Do not miss the deadline or your LLC will be dissolved.

Mississippi

Domestic filing fee: $50

Renewal: $0

Foreign filing fee: $250

Entity name must contain "Limited Liability Company", or any abbreviation thereof. Standard filing procedure, operating agreement is required and may be verbal or written, but highly recommended to maintain a written file. Both foreign and domestic LLC's must file an annual report due between January 1st and April 15th.

Missouri

Domestic filing fee: $105 by paper, $50 online

Renewal: $0

Foreign filing fee: $105

Entity name must contain "Limited Liability Company", or any abbreviation thereof. Standard filing procedure, operating agreement not required, but highly recommended to maintain a written file. Both foreign and domestic LLC's do not need to file an annual report.

Montana

Domestic filing fee: $70 + $50 for each additional member in a series LLC

Renewal: $20

Foreign filing fee: $70 + $50 for each additional member in a series LLC

Expedited fee: $100

Entity name must contain "Limited Liability Company", or any abbreviation thereof. Standard filing procedure, operating agreement is required and may be verbal or written, but highly recommended to maintain a written file. Both foreign and domestic LLC's must file an annual report due April 15th.

Nebraska

Domestic filing fee: $100 + $10 for the certificate

Renewal: $10 on paper, $13 online

Foreign filing fee: $100 + $10 for the certificate

Entity name must contain "Limited Liability Company", or any abbreviation thereof. Standard filing procedure, notice of organization is required for 3 consecutive weeks in newspaper of general circulation, and an operating must be filed with the state. Both foreign and domestic LLC's must file a biennial report due April 1st in odd years.

Nevada

Domestic filing fee: $75

Renewal: $10

Foreign filing fee: $75

Expedite fee: $125

Entity name must contain "Limited Liability Company", or any abbreviation thereof including "Ltd.". Standard filing procedure, with exception of an operating agreement is not required to be filed with the state, however it is highly recommended you do keep one on file. Both foreign and domestic LLC's must file a report every year by the end of the month of the anniversary date of the formation of the LLC.

New Hampshire

Domestic filing fee: $100, $50 for certificate of formation

Renewal: $100

Foreign filing fee: $100

Entity name must include Limited Liability Company, Ltd. Liability Company, or any abbreviation thereof. Standard filing procedure, an operating agreement is not required to be filed, it is highly advisable to keep this on file. Both foreign and domestic LLC's must file a report every year by April 1st.

New Jersey

Domestic filing fee: $125

Renewal: $50

Foreign filing fee: $125

Expedited fee: $25 per filing, $50 same day

Entity name must include Limited Liability Company, Ltd. Liability Company, or an abbreviation thereof. Standard filing procedure, an operating agreement is not required to be filed with state, but it is highly advisable to keep this on file. Both foreign and domestic LLC's must file a report every year, due at the end of the month of the anniversary date the LLC was formed.

New Mexico

Domestic filing fee: $50

Renewal: $0

Foreign filing fee: $100

Entity name must include Limited Liability Company, Ltd. Liability Company, or an abbreviation thereof. Standard filing procedure, an operating agreement is not required to be filed with state, but it is highly advisable to keep this on file. Both foreign and domestic LLC's are not required to file an annual report.

New York

Domestic filing fee: $200

Renewal: $9

Foreign filing fee: $250

Entity name must include Limited Liability Company, Ltd. Liability Company, or an abbreviation thereof. Standard filing procedure, a proof of publication must be completed within 120 days of formation of an LLC and must be published in both a daily and weekly and must be designated by the county clerk in the county which the LLC is located. An operating agreement may be verbal or written and must be filed with the state. Both foreign and domestic LLC's are required to file a biennial report and due by the end of the month within every other anniversary date in which the LLC was formed. Late fees are hefty at $250.

North Carolina

Domestic filing fee: $125

Renewal: $200

Foreign filing fee: $250

Entity name must contain "Limited Liability Company", or any abbreviation thereof. Standard filing procedure, an operating agreement is not required but it is highly recommended you keep one on file. Both foreign and domestic LLC's must file an annual report due every year on April 15th.

North Dakota

Domestic filing fee: $135

Renewal: $50

Foreign filing fee: $135

Entity name must contain "Limited Liability Company", or any abbreviation thereof. Standard filing procedure, operating agreement not required, but highly recommended to maintain a written file. Both foreign and domestic LLC's must file an annual report due every year on November 15th; first-year LLC are due within a year of formation.

Ohio

Domestic filing fee: $99

Foreign filing fee: $99

Expedited fee: $100

Entity name must contain "Limited Liability Company", or any abbreviation thereof. Standard filing procedure, an operating agreement is not required but it is highly recommended you keep one on file. Both foreign and domestic LLC's do not need to file an annual report.

Oregon

Domestic filing fee: $100

Renewal: $100

Foreign filing fee: $275

Entity name must contain "Limited Liability Company", or any abbreviation thereof. Standard filing procedure, an operating agreement is not required but it is highly recommended you keep one on file. Both foreign and domestic LLC's must file an annual report, due by the anniversary date in which the LLC was formed.

Pennsylvania

Domestic filing fee: $125

Renewal: $500

Foreign filing fee: $250

Expedited fee: $

Entity name must contain "Limited Liability Company", or any abbreviation thereof. Standard filing procedure, an operating agreement is not required but it is highly recommended you keep one on file. Both foreign and domestic LLC's must file a report every ten years, due by the anniversary date in which the LLC was formed.

Rhode Island

Domestic filing fee: $150

Renewal: $50

Foreign filing fee: $150

Entity name must contain "Limited Liability Company", or any abbreviation thereof. Standard filing procedure, an operating agreement is not required but it is highly recommended you keep one on file. Both foreign and domestic LLC's must file an annual report, due by between September 1st and November 1st.

South Carolina

Domestic filing fee: $110

Foreign filing fee: $110

Entity name must contain "Limited Liability Company", or any abbreviation thereof. Standard filing procedure, an operating agreement is not required but it is highly recommended you keep one on file. Both foreign and domestic LLC's do not need to file an annual report.

South Dakota

Domestic filing fee: $150 if filed online, $165 if filed on paper

Renewal: $50 filed online, $65 of filed on paper

Foreign filing fee: $150 if filed online, $165 if filed on paper

Entity name must contain "Limited Liability Company", or any abbreviation thereof. Standard filing procedure, an operating agreement is not required but it is highly recommended you keep one on file. Both foreign and domestic LLC's must file an annual report due by November 15th, first-year LLC's must file by the anniversary date in which the LLC was formed.

Tennessee

Domestic filing fee: $300 minimum, $50 per member up to a maximum of $3,000

Renewal: $300 minimum, $50 per member up to a maximum of $3,000

Foreign filing fee: $300 minimum, $50 per member up to a maximum of $3,000

Entity name must contain "Limited Liability Company", or any abbreviation thereof. Standard filing procedure, an operating agreement is not required but it is highly recommended you keep one on file. Both foreign and domestic LLC's must file an annual report, due by the first day of the fourth month following the close of the LLC's fiscal year.

Texas

Domestic filing fee: $300

Renewal: If revenues below $110,000 no fee, if above fees are due on a graduated scale

Foreign filing fee: $750

Entity name must contain "Limited Liability Company", or any abbreviation thereof. Standard filing procedure, an operating agreement is not required but it is highly recommended you keep one on file. Both foreign and domestic LLC's must file an annual report that is due May 15th, but not due in the first year an LLC was formed, for instance if a company was formed on April 1, 2017, the annual report would be due May 15, 2018.

Utah

Domestic filing fee: $70

Renewal: $15

Foreign filing fee: $70

Expedited fee: $75

Entity name must contain "Limited Liability Company", or any abbreviation thereof. Standard filing procedure, an operating agreement is not required but it is highly recommended you keep one on file. Both foreign and domestic LLC's must file an annual report, due by the anniversary date in which the LLC was formed.

Vermont

Domestic filing fee: $125

Renewal: $35, $140 for foreign

Foreign filing fee: $125

Entity name must contain "Limited Liability Company", or any abbreviation thereof. Standard filing procedure, an operating agreement is not required but it is highly recommended you keep one on file. Both foreign and domestic LLC's must file an annual report, due within two and a half months following the end of an LLC's fiscal year.

Virginia

Domestic filing fee: $100

Renewal: $50

Foreign filing fee: $120

Entity name must contain "Limited Liability Company", or any abbreviation thereof. Standard filing procedure, an operating agreement is not required but it is highly recommended you keep one on file. Both foreign and domestic LLC's must file an annual report, due on the first of the second month following the anniversary date of the formation of the LLC.

Washington

Domestic filing fee: $180 by paper, $200 online

Renewal: $250 by paper, $300 if filed online

Foreign filing fee: $200 online only

Entity name must contain "Limited Liability Company", or any abbreviation thereof. Standard filing procedure, an operating agreement is not required but it is highly recommended you keep one on file. Both foreign and domestic LLC's must file an annual report, an initial report is due within 120 days of forming the LLC, and annually due by the month's end within the anniversary of the formation of the LLC.

Washington D.C.

Domestic filing fee: $220, walk-ins charged an additional $100

Renewal: $300

Foreign filing fee: $220

Entity name must contain "Limited Liability Company", or any abbreviation thereof. Standard filing procedure, an operating agreement is not required but it is highly recommended you keep one on file. Both foreign and domestic LLC's must file a biennial report due on April 1st. New companies must also file an initial report a year after formation on April 1st.

West Virginia

Domestic filing fee: $100

Renewal: $25

Foreign filing fee: $150

Entity name must contain "Limited Liability Company", or any abbreviation thereof. Standard filing procedure, an operating agreement is not required but it is highly recommended you keep one on file. Both foreign and domestic LLC's must file an annual report, due by June 30th.

Wisconsin

Domestic filing fee: $130 online, $170 by paper

Renewal: $25 domestic, $80 foreign

Foreign filing fee: $130 online, $170 by paper

Entity name must contain "Limited Liability Company", or any abbreviation thereof. Standard filing procedure, an operating agreement is not required but it is highly recommended you keep one on file. Both foreign and domestic LLC's must file an annual report, due by the end of the quarter within the anniversary date the LLC was formed.

Wyoming

Domestic filing fee: $100

Renewal: $50 or .02% of the value of all assets, whichever is greater

Foreign filing fee: $100

Entity name must contain "Limited Liability Company", or any abbreviation thereof. Standard filing procedure, an operating agreement is not required but it is highly recommended you keep one on file. Both foreign and domestic LLC's must file an annual report, due by the first of the month within the anniversary of the LLC's formation, for example an LLC formed on the 12th of July would file the following year by the 1st of July. First-year LLC's do not have to file an annual report.

It is important that all LLC's file their reports where and when required, on time. A late fee may apply. In some cases, a state may dissolve your company immediately, in others there may be up to a two-year delay. Mark these filing dates on a calendar or however you set reminders.

Chapter 6 – LLC Hiring Tips

Hiring for your business may also be a priority. If your business is new or even if you are established, understanding best hiring practices will not only help in getting the right staff but will help alleviate potential problems. There are compliance requirements and, of course, your goals for the new hire.

On the compliance side, the IRS requires every new hire to complete a W-4 form. The W-4 is for determining federal tax withholding amounts. Your state may also have a similar form. Form I-9 is used for verification purposes of every new hire. This form is filled by both citizens and non-citizens and outlines required identification used for verification purposes. The next step is to report to your state's employment agency about your new hire. This may be a form or conducted online. The final step is to report the new hire on your worker's compensation insurance policy.

On the practical side, it is important you define the role for which you are hiring. Are you looking for an office manager who may cover many tasks, or just a cashier to greet customers and do basic shop-keeping duties? Defining the role and outlining duties and responsibilities is your first priority. The next step is to research what would be fair pay for this new role. You can do research on websites for similar positions in your area, or you may be able to just do a job search to get an idea of what your competitors are paying. If you have a budget and it is below the normal rate in your area you may have a difficult time filling the position depending on the state of the local job market. Having some payroll budget flexibility might be a good idea, for many business owners fail to understand the training and acquisition costs every new hire costs. Consider even a cashier position. A training session could take a couple of hours, which means another employee is dedicating his or her working time to get the new hire up to speed. An administrator, maybe even you, will have to spend time with some type of indoctrination process, including filling out required paperwork and giving the new hire a tour of the facilities and answering any questions. That will easily consume 1-2 hours of time. There's the cost of posting the ad for that new hire in addition to time for you or a manager to interview prospective employees for the position, which could easily consume an entire workday. At this point, we're at 11-12 hours of time spent on this new hire, plus advertising costs, if any. Now consider the new hire may also need a uniform or perhaps some safety equipment. This also has costs, and there is lost productivity from the actual training and administrative time committed to the learning time for the new employee to become proficient. Customer service and errors, as with most new employees mistakes may happen. For example, say the new cashier doesn't understand the policy on customer returns and mistakenly gives a customer cash back instead of giving store credit. Another example would be a new hire just getting used to the new role and your expectations when dealing with customers. A new employee may not have the same level of understanding on what is proper when dealing with new customers and this can also hurt your brand. The final consideration is cultural impact – a new employee is at the least a welcome addition, but every new employee goes through an acclimation process. If the new hire is replacing someone, for whatever reason, your other employees may question why; if this is a frequent occurrence, your company culture may suffer. It is important for any manager to understand why retention is a problem and understand the costs of constantly replacing employees, even at the most basic level.

Hiring employees can consume much of any person's time. Whether you are posting a sign on your door, asking your team or friends for referrals, using social media to find talent, or have a decent advertising budget, you will have to spend time crafting these ads to make sure you're getting quality candidates. You may get flooded with resumes and weeding through these submissions can take time, and unless you rely on sophisticated software to scan for keywords, you could easily spend an entire workday trying to find that perfect candidate or at least narrow it down to handful of quality individuals. Now that you've narrowed a few candidates down, you've got to coordinate interview times and block some time for those sessions. After the interviews, you must now further refine whom you would like to hire. You may present an offer, they counter with perhaps asking for more pay, you agree, and then it turns out he or she got a better offer from your competitor across town, back to the candidate list. Rinse, repeat.

We brushed up on training, but there are some important factors to remember with a new hire: your objectives and the new employee's level of understanding and making sure to bridge the gap between those two. As a new employee gets into the training cycle, it is important to listen as they may have new approaches to doing things and he or she may have prior experience that could prove to be a timesaver. Allowing the new employee to express ideas also gives empowerment and shows that you are open to improvement. Make sure you don't neglect senior employees, and make sure they understand that they should also be involved in the new hire's development and potentially be a mentor. It goes without saying, you should take time to give feedback to correct mistakes as they happen and coach the new hire, at the same time you should also set clear goals. Also allow your new hire to interact with other members of your team; this will allow the new hire to feel like part of the team and create potential bonds with others. In the end, reward and recognize improvement and accomplishing goals - these little instances of encouragement can lead to a more cohesive work environment and make work a positive experience.

Hiring, training, and retaining new team members is key to any business. Once you identify top talent, it is in your best interest to keep them, develop them, recognize them, or risk losing them. It is critical that any member understands the costs of turnover and identify opportunities within your own processes that can reduce losing employees and ultimately create a rewarding workplace.

Chapter 7 – LLC Accounting Explained

Accounting in an LLC is not much different than accounting for any other type of business. A member must decide what method of accounting to use, preferred inventory method, and be sure to keep a detailed ledger of all transactions incurred. Another consideration are internal controls to be utilized.

A company must determine what accounting period they want maintain: they can follow the calendar year, or they can elect a fiscal year which is a one-year period that may or may not follow the calendar year. For instance, a company may want to end their fiscal year on June 30th due to a natural slowdown in the selling cycle. The fiscal year end could allow for a short period to account for inventory and conduct a cycle count where all inventory is manually counted and recorded in the books. A company must be aware that once a fiscal year is selected, it is difficult to switch to another accounting period.

There are two methods of accounting, cash and accrual. Both are acceptable for use in an LLC, but accrual will yield more accurate financials. The key difference between the two methods is that in accrual accounting revenues are recognized when earned such as entering a sale on credit, and expenses are recognized when they incur like entering a bill that may not be due for another couple of weeks. As you can imagine with the cash method, revenues are recognized when cash is received, and when expenses are actually paid. There is more complexity involved with the accrual method including accruing expenses and payroll or prepayments for expenses such as insurance where the annual premium is paid upfront. Cash accounting is much simpler in process and only limited staff is needed to make entries. It doesn't require in-depth knowledge to implement.

The standard accounting system used in a majority of businesses in the United States and has been around for at least 500 years. It is known as double-entry accounting. There is a system known as single-entry accounting, similar to keeping track of transactions in a check register where you get deposits and record expenses from a single account. This system is rarely used in business other than where there may be only a limited number of transactions in a given period. For the extent of this chapter we will be dealing with double-entry accounting, more appropriate for a more complex business and obviously an LLC. In double-entry accounting every transaction involves at least two accounts which maintains balance on the balance sheet. For instance, a purchase of a laptop involves debiting the computer assets account while crediting cash in bank (both an asset account is increased while another asset account decreases which results in no net change on the balance sheet). Paying a vendor bill involves debiting accounts payable (the liability amount goes up) while crediting cash (an asset amount goes down). Of course, the entry of the bill also involves two accounts, and in the end strives to maintain balance on the balance sheet. Accounting software can automatically account for this using the proper module in the software and makes bookkeeping easy.

It is important for any business owner to understand the basic accounting equation of Assets = Liabilities + Equity. Assets can include cash, inventory, prepaid expenses, and accounts receivable. A liability is any debt owed to a creditor or vendor, salaries payable, or any consumer deposit. Equity includes member contributions and any retained earnings. These three elements make up the balance sheet of a business and accounting software makes sure transactions allocate how money paid or taken in affects the balance sheet and profit and loss statements. As your business grows it may be wise to invest in accounting software and a good program can grow with it. Another option may be to hire an outside firm to maintain your books. There are many programs available, from software to cloud-based systems which can aid certain types of businesses such as companies with field representatives or consultants that can aid in tracking expenses and mileage on-the-go. At the basic level, accounting software can produce financial reporting that can help a business owner or manager better understand how a business is performing, on a higher level this reporting can assist a business owner or manager in growing his or her business such as obtaining a loan or attracting investors.

Part of understanding accounting for a manager is also understanding your chart of accounts. Basic accounting software may allow a template set up, depending on the type of business you have. Some ready-made account setups might include a restaurant or a service provider. For example, a consultant wouldn't have too much inventory or not very many costs of goods sold accounts, as opposed to a manufacturer, who may have several accounts for inventory, including work in progress or finished goods along with costs of goods sold for each type of product produced. Your chart of accounts will include the assets, liabilities and equity included above. The beauty of software is it allows you to add accounts or make accounts obsolete as your needs change. It is important to keep track of these accounts and update them every time your business grows, or contracts, for that matter.

Sales or income is what almost every business strives for. A consultant may provide expertise in the form of billable hours to a client, a retailer provides goods for consumers at a mark-up, or a utility provider may provide water for a customer for personal or business use. All these transfers of goods from business to consumer or business to business are sales. Sales can be paid for immediately or on credit (discussed in the next paragraph). As cash is received for these goods or services, it increases your cash in bank balance and income is received and recorded on the profit and loss statement.

A statement of cash flows is another report important for any business owner. This report shows how cash is generated and spent in a given period. The first portion of the statement of cash flows are operating activities. These include cash payments to suppliers, cash payments to employees, cash payments for taxes, and cash refunds to customers. Cash flows from investing activities are cash from the sales of long-term investments or of land or equipment. Financing activities derive from the issuance or repurchase of a company's stocks or bonds and the payment of dividends. Supplemental information could include other activities such as payment of income taxes or interest paid, or any significant transaction where an exchange was made but no cash was involved.

Accounts receivable, as mentioned above, is an asset account where goods are sold to prospective customers. You may choose to extend credit to those customers in which they receive an invoice, the balance of these invoices is recorded on the accounts receivable balance. As these invoices are paid, payment is received, lowering the accounts receivable balance and increasing sales. Both these transactions are booked and recorded on the balance sheet, as well as shown as an increase on the income portion of the profit and loss statement.

Purchases are part of a business, whether it is for actual equipment used for the business only or for raw materials used as part of an assembly for a finished good of a manufacturer. In this instance we are referring to purchases made for resale to consumers or as part of manufacturing process. We'll discuss more about these purchases and the accounting of them in the next paragraph.

Inventory valuation and accounting for it properly are also considerations for a retail or manufacturing business. Inventory valuation is important as assets in a warehouse or on your shelves are booked onto a balance sheet. These goods are tracked as cost of goods and when sold or counted as revenues. Having an accurate gauge on these aspects can aid in decision-making for a business owner. Inventory accounting methods are either perpetual, where goods are tracked constantly as they are sold or when inventory is added, or periodic, where sales may be recorded as they occur, but inventory isn't necessarily updated at the same time and physical inventory must be conducted to update cost of goods sold (COGS). Types of inventory also includes products that may not be fully assembled. These goods are known as work in progress (WIP). For instance, a company may manufacture robotic arms; however, a supplier is experiencing delays and is unable to ship a circuit board needed to complete assembly. These unfinished goods would be set aside and booked as WIP. Finished goods are just the opposite as these goods are ready for sale and booked into that inventory account.

If using the perpetual system of accounting, one must also decide what method to determine cost of goods sold and how to value that. The three most common methods include:

1. First-in, first-out (FIFO)- the oldest items in inventory are recorded sold first (not physically, but for costing purposes). For example, a company receives 200 units of Item A at $50, in a later shipment they receive 100 units Item A at $30, and a final shipment of 50 units of Item A at $40. The company sells 310 units of Item A, so the cost of goods sold would be: $(200 \times \$50) + (100 \times \$30) + (10 \times \$40) = \$13,400$

2. Last-in, first-out (LIFO)- the latest items in inventory are recorded as sold first (for costing purposes). For example: ABC Jelly receives 50 units of Item B on January 1 at $10, 25 units of Item B on January 31 at $20, and 20 units of Item

B on February 15 at $15. ABC Jelly records 50 units of Item B sold on February 28. The cost of goods sold would be calculated: (20 x $15) + (25 x $20) + (5 x $10) = $850

3. Average cost or weighted average cost- this method disregards receipt dates and simply accounts for a weighted average cost for items in inventory at any given time. For instance, ABC Jelly has the same shipment quantities and costs from the LIFO example above, the weighted average cost for these items would be: $500 + $500 + $300 = $1,300/95 units = $13.68 per unit. ABC Jelly sells 65 units in the month of March, weighted average costs of sales is: 65 x $13.68 = $889.20

It is also important to discuss how cost of goods are accounted for and the simplest way to explain this is through the equation: COGS= beginning inventory + purchases made during the accounting period – ending inventory. The beginning inventory may be 25 sofas for furniture retailer at $400 each, the retailer may purchase ten more sofas at $450, and sell 30 sofas valued at $450, the cost of goods sold would be (25 x $400) + (10 x $450) – (30 x $450) = $1,000. This figure would be recorded on the profit and loss statement and subtracted from income. Accounts payable where vendors extend credit to you as a business or are expenses booked and due at a later date. Such an expense would be a bill for your electricity. When the bill is received it is booked into the accounting system along with the due date. This increases your accounts payable balance. Once the bill is paid this decreases the accounts payable balance while decreasing your cash in bank balance. This is also reflected on the profit and loss statement where this increases your expense balance and lowers your profit or increase losses.

Loans payable may also be an account that may need to be maintained. A bank may extend credit to a business. This may extend many years, such as a business loan or even a vehicle loan. A loan that extends longer than one year is considered a long-term liability. The loan is booked when it is obtained as a long-term liability and as payments are made this both decreases the liability balance while decreasing the cash in bank balance. The only expense recorded that will reflect on the profit and loss statement is any interest expense paid.

Members of an LLC should also understand the difference between an allocation and a distribution. Allocations are tied to an LLC's profits and losses, distributions are tied to both income and member contributions. It is important to account for a member's contributed capital separately and distribute income or losses at the end of each period. It is also important these are distributed equally and in proportion to each member's contribution to ensure that each member is reporting the proper amount of income or losses to the proper taxing authorities.

Payroll accounting is also important for any business. Even in a single-member LLC with no employees it is important for that single member to keep track of detailed expenses from meals to mileage driving to clients in the course of business and to be sure he or she is maximizing deductions. In a company with additional employees, you may elect to handle payroll yourself and while this can reduce expenses, it can add more duties and complexity for someone within the company who must report earnings to the federal and state agencies. These filings must be reported following every pay date, and any error can equate to hefty fees if an error is discovered by the taxing authority.

Retained earnings are also important for a business. These are earnings surplus at the end of an accounting period not distributed to members of an LLC. These earnings are reinvested into a business and may be used to acquire additional equipment, purchase additional inventory, improve facilities, or these earnings may be invested in short-term bonds or other type of investment in order to grow that money while reducing the tax burden of a business. All retained earnings are recorded on the balance sheet. Most purchases used for business improvements would also be recorded on a balance sheet, with perhaps some expenses, such as freight and taxes paid for purchases, which would be recorded as an expense.

Internal controls are also essential for a growing business. As your company grows and more employees are added, internal controls become easier to implement. For instance, a small family-owned retailer may have limited staff and only a few personnel handling cash in the register. As your staff grows and more shifts are added, it makes accountability more difficult. End of shift cash counting may be handled by the same person who is the cashier in a family business. Now, as you add outside employees, it might be wise to have one person operating a register and a manager or supervisor counting cash at the end of a shift. Another internal control is for booking payroll. For instance, one employee may cut checks for weekly payroll, but another person should verify entries. As a company grows it could be very easy to lose track of new employees or even departing employees for that matter, this opens up an opportunity for a fake employee to be added to the payroll, a terminated employee to be left on the books, or for a pay-rate to be inflated. With a second person verifying check disbursement amounts, this closes the opportunity for dishonesty.

A last word of caution is for audits. An audit can be conducted by the IRS or even a local tax authority. For an IRS audit, they will be looking at not only how your books appear, but will also be sizing up the member or members of a company. If your tax returns make it appear that you generate little income or profit, yet every manager is driving a high-end, European luxury sedan, it may be time to dig deeper into a company's books to be sure all that is being recorded. If your business deals with lots of cash, such as a restaurant, it may raises suspicion that skimming is occurring and income is not being recorded properly. If you have only one car and are a consultant, was mileage properly logged? This is where keeping a mileage log and detailed invoicing can prove your case. If you wrote off season tickets to a local sports team, be sure you can provide proof that you attended the games for business purposes, such as entertaining clients. Be careful as your LLC is at risk when you start to write off what seemingly may be innocent, but a sharp-eyed auditor may see an unusual charge, like an expensive purchase at a fancy retailer, and may want to see a receipt. A final warning: be sure your independent contractors are truly independent; if you are dictating their schedules, and the individual is not invoicing for the work completed, those may be indicators that you have an employee not an independent contractor.

You should understand your business needs and when to hire accounting staff or seek outside help to help maintain your books. Having a knowledgeable staff member can allow for ready access to reports, immediate booking of transactions, and the ability to keep tabs on cash flows to better help you make strategic decisions. As your company grows, additional staff and duties may be required, such as separating accounts payables and receivables, and even more growth may result in the need of a supervisor or even a controller to keep tabs of more complex accounting situations where there are multiple divisions or significant volume of both revenues and transactions. Here are common accounting positions within companies starting from with the lowest-level position and continuing all the way up to CFO:

1. Accounting clerk- maintains and produces financial records within a company,

2. Accountant/staff accountant- Maintains, prepares, and analyzes financial records for a business. May have other duties such as managing payroll, taxes and payables or receivables,

3. Auditor- similar duties to an accountant, but also has additional skills or verifying transactions follow procedures as set forth by general accepted accounting procedures (GAAP) as well as maintaining internal controls,

4. Financial analyst- Evaluates businesses and projects through modeling and computer simulations to determine if something is worth investing in,

5. Controller- Responsible for all accounting activities within an organization. This individual may also prepare budgets, financial statements, and prepare taxes. Reports to the CFO,

6. Chief financial officer (CFO)- Manages all financing activities within an organization. Manages all facets of accounting and reports to the CEO on the overall financial state of a company through reports and analysis.

Accounting is an essential part of any business and essential in most cases for an LLC. It is best to understand inventory, internal controls, and how to keep detailed records to aid in decision making and to ensure operations run smoothly. Accounting can be accomplished internally through software or even handled by a third-party. Most importantly, embrace the habit of keeping detailed records and accounting will be easier and be one less worry for a member or owner.

Chapter 8 – LLC Taxes

As Ben Franklin said, the only certainty in life is death and taxes. Taxes are inevitable when dealing with any type of business. In an LLC there are certain considerations that must be adhered to and understood to be sure you're getting the most for deductions and to be sure you're in compliance. It is also important to identify how taxes with an LLC differ from the other types of business entities.

As mentioned previously, tax filings are flexible. Depending on the management structure of your LLC, single-member LLC files as it would be a for a sole proprietorship, and a multi-member LLC files as if it was a partnership. An LLC is a pass-through entity, so each member must report profits and losses on their individual tax returns. It is important to remember that in a multi-member LLC, each partner must report their share of profits or losses as outlined in their share of ownership. For instance, Jill owns 60% of ABC Jelly, LLC, Jack owns 40% and the company generated $100,000 in profits last year, so Jill would claim $60,000 of the profit as income, and Jack would claim the remaining $40,0000. Also, a multi-member LLC must file its own Form 1065 to report how profits or losses were distributed amongst members. This is a form of checks and balances for the IRS so it's important that each member report matching numbers to avoid triggering an audit. If you are a new LLC or one whose business is winding down and you have no business activity, you still must file your taxes on the appropriate forms with the IRS.

A final consideration with taxes is the option for an LLC to elect being subject to corporate taxation. In such a case, the LLC files a Form 8832 with the IRS, and then selects the appropriate corporate tax treatment option. Starting in 2018, it can also be advantageous for an LLC to be taxed as a "C" corporation. It is taxed at a flat 21% compared to filing as an individual or partner, for which the rate can range from 32% to 37%. These profits, when taxed as a corporation, are considered retained earnings. One should also be aware that even though these profits are taxed at a low rate, money distributed to members are subject to additional taxes via double taxation, but these rates are still taxed lower than filing as an individual or partnership. These earnings are considered capital gains and only subject to a 23.8% tax rate. Filing as a corporation also opens other methods to pass down tax-advantaged fringe benefits, such as stock options or stock ownership plans, which in either case aren't subject to double taxation.

Income taxes for members of an LLC are not subject to regular income tax and are treated the same as self-employed individuals. With this in mind, members must file a quarterly estimate of their earnings. These filings are due in April, June, September, and January. A word of caution with filing taxes: do not be late! The IRS penalizes partnerships a hefty $195 per member, so for a 10-member partnership filing 6 months late that would be $11,700 total.

Self-employment taxes are also something to be considered for a member of an LLC. Much like sole-proprietorships or partnerships, owners are not subject to typical payroll withholdings such as Social Security and Medicare taxes. Instead, a member must file a Schedule SE. This annual filing is taxed at a rate of 15.3% up to a certain threshold, after that an additional 2.9% is levied on those earnings.

Much like any business, expenses and deductions are plentiful for an LLC. These expenses can range from vehicle and travel expenses, start-up costs, depreciation expenses, supplies, and advertising costs which will lower your profits, and these expenses may be "written off."

State taxes where applicable are also to be considered by a member of an LLC.   The individual pays taxes as one is required. Additionally, an LLC may also be subject to state taxes based upon its earnings. For example, California charges a tax if an LLC makes more than $250,000 per year. Another example is Florida, where an LLC can fit into various tax rates depending how the LLC files taxes with the IRS, an individual-member LLC is not subject to income taxes, a partnership pays partnership taxes, and if filing as a corporation, that LLC pays the corporate tax rate. Check your state laws or consult with a tax expert before filing any state taxes.

The Tax Cuts and Jobs Act has opened new loopholes in how entrepreneurs may want to claim income. The IRS hasn't created too many regulations for preventing tax avoiding strategies, and here are some tactics that may help you take advantage of these lax regulations (always consult with a tax professional before taking such measures). First, this is a 20% deduction allowed for pass-through incomes of "S" corporations and LLC's, of course and is valid for 2018. The income caps for a single taxpayer: Your income must be below $157,500, or $315,000 if you're married or in a domestic partnership and filing jointly.

The first strategy is to use an asset to create a new LLC; for instance, a married chiropractor makes more than $315,000 per year Now if the chiropractor were to separate his practice, ABC Chiropractic, Inc., from the building he owns, and create Backpain Office Leasing, Inc, the chiropractor could charge an annual lease of $300,000 per year to qualify for the deduction for both entities.

Another loophole is a small business in which the reputation or skill of an employee is considered a service and therefore is not entitled to the 20% deduction. Now say a celebrity opens a new restaurant with his name on the place. Will the restaurant pin its profits on the reputation of the owner or the quality of their food? This is a topic for debate and savvy owners will be able to claim what is proper to get that deduction.

The final loophole includes saving for retirement. Say a single entrepreneur made $200,000 last year. She wouldn't qualify for the deduction, but she could sock away that excess $42,500 and put it into a defined contribution plan. For 2018 the limit is $55,000, which includes 401(k) plans.

These three loopholes can help you maximize your deductions to stay ahead of the new tax law. Be sure to consult your tax professional to see if any or all of these scenarios will work with your situation.

We also discussed state fees and it's worth reminding that these fees are often due annually. These fees are called all sorts of names, from "franchise tax," "renewal fee," or "registration fee," but make no mistake - it's a cost of doing business. As always, check with your state regulator to determine what your fee is and when it is due.

Chapter 9 – Transitioning an Existing Business into an LLC

At this point, perhaps you feel an LLC may be the right type of entity for you. If you are starting fresh, no need to read this chapter, but if you already have an existing business either for yourself, or as part of a partnership, there are considerations you must make. We've discussed the process and tax advantages, but making a change is difficult for everyone involved in an organization and even more so for the owners and managers.

For a sole proprietorship, the process is much like starting an LLC from scratch. Consider a sole proprietor who is a business consultant. Perhaps when Joan was consulting, she was filing her 1099 forms with the IRS, but never actually filed with the state that she was an actual business entity. In this case, Joan never had a business entity, and it would be best for her to start fresh as an LLC if she wishes to shield her personal assets. You might be able to use your original name and tack on limited liability company, or LLC, to your existing company name and file that new name with the state regulator. It is imperative to conduct a business name search to verify your business name will work as an LLC. As mentioned in Chapter 2, you will need a registered agent and file your articles of organization with the state. The other two big changes when converting to an LLC from a sole proprietorship are filing for a new employee identification number (EIN) with the Internal Revenue

Service and opening a new account. If you keep the same name or re-invent yourself, your new EIN will have that all-important LLC on your paperwork. Once that is approved, you will need to open an entirely new account with your chosen bank. This is not only required, but even more importantly, can separate transactions where perhaps your previous business account may have covered some personal expenses. It is important to keep clear, separate transactions of business expenses away from personal expenses with the new account to avoid piercing the corporate veil. With the new account in mind, you should close the old bank account.

As for transitioning from a partnership to an LLC, the process is much the same as for a sole proprietorship with some key differences. The articles of organization will be slightly different in that each member or manager must have his or her responsibilities outlined for day-to-day management. Another difference with having one or more owners: a partnership's existing assets must be transferred to the LLC. The easiest way to accomplish this is by creating a bill of sale for the assets, assigning a value, then making the LLC the owner of these items. You will next need to shut down the partnership in the state which you conduct business. This is accomplished with a Certificate of Cancellation. Of course, if there was no formal agreement in the beginning, a cancellation notice may not be required.

A final consideration is whether to convert a corporation to an LLC. This may sound counter-intuitive, but companies desiring more management freedom may find this a better option. One must weigh the result of a hefty tax bill before even considering this move. Of course, it is important to remember the difference in how each type of entity is operated. A corporation must have a board of directors, where an LLC can have a less formal management structure with much more freedom in operation and decision-making processes. Distributing profits in an LLC is also much less formalized and not determined by the number of shares owned as in a corporation. A historical example of a corporation transitioning to an LLC would be Daimler Chrysler AG. In 2007, over 80% of shares were sold to a private equity firm, Cerberus Capital Management, at which point Chrysler LLC was formed. Another example of this is Burger King, which technically has been privatized twice; the latest happened in 2014 when it merged with Tim Hortons, a Canadian-based, multi-national coffee and donut franchise.

Chapter 10 – Dissolution of an LLC

Much like establishing an LLC, there are steps to formalize the dissolution or sale of a limited liability company. There comes a time when an end might be the best course of action or you may be ready to sell your stake in ownership and pass it along to another member or a third party. Sometimes the owner may want to retire, other times a business has run its course and its time to close the business.

If you plan to sell your LLC, it can be a complex process coming up with a value for the company. This is where a business valuation expert can accurately look at all facets of your business to determine what is fair for not only the assets, liabilities, and equity stakes of your business but also for the brand itself. A potential buyer may not even be interested in the entire business, but may just want the assets, a valuation expert can help parcel out appraisals as well.

A sale is not straightforward as there are not only filings that must be handled with the state, but also tax implications. It is best to hire a lawyer to make sure all matters are settled before executing a sale. Once you handle these matters, a memorandum of understanding is likely the first step a member or members and the potential buyer will enter before executing a formal contract.

The first step is granting approval to dissolve the LLC. Members must approve the decision. It is often easy for members to understand the reason for closing as they are involved in day to day operations, but passive members may not be in the loop so be prepared to show financials or justify a stance. A good step in this process is to document the decision and make sure all members sign the document agreeing to end the business.

The next step is to file the proper paperwork with the state or with other states for those with foreign LLC's. Often referred to as the articles of dissolution, this formally announces to the state your wish to no longer operate as an entity. In some states the announcement can be made prior to settling debts and resolving claims, in others these affairs must be resolved before filing. Another requirement may be that a tax clearance must be authorized before a dissolution is approved.

Tax forms and tax authorities also need to be notified. You must notify the IRS of the closing of your business. Your state and local taxing agencies may also require notification. To simplify the process and then be sure you're in compliance, it may be best to have your tax representative or accountant assist with this process.

Creditors will also need to be officially notified of your business closing. This must be accomplished by mail and must include: your intent to dissolve the LLC, a mailing address to for which to they can send their claims, and a deadline to submit said claims (it also explains any claims submitted after the deadline will be barred). You may additionally be required to file a notice of dissolution with a publisher. As always, when in doubt, seek legal advice or refer to your state's commerce website for guidance.

Settling claims with creditors is also required. If your business is closing due to insolvency, a creditor may agree to accept less than the owed amount. In these cases, get the agreed amount in writing along with an outline of terms on how the debt will be settled. You may also reject any claims, but you must notify the creditor in writing of this objection. A lawyer may be necessary in advising how to resolve disputed claims and how to best proceed regarding your state's laws.

The final step is distributing assets. With a single member LLC, the process is straightforward. In the case of a multi-member LLC, ownership stakes should be considered. In our ABC Jelly LLC example, recall that Jill owns 60% of the business and Jack owns 40%. Once all debts are settled, the remaining assets can be split amongst both members in this same proportion. These distributions are then reported to the IRS.

Ending a business is always a tough decision even under the happiest of terms. As long as the member, or members, of an LLC follow these steps and consult with proper tax, legal, or state agencies when necessary, ending an LLC can be methodical, in compliance with state laws, and the process can be made less stressful.

Conclusion

Now that you understand what an LLC is, how it works, and the process for forming one, you can now make an informed decision to determine if it's the right type of business entity for you. Each person must weigh their financial position, his/her exposure to risk, and think strategically as to whether or not an LLC would make sense for his or her organization. It is certainly not a one-size fits all solution ,and may not be the best business type either from a tax standpoint, or even from a legal standpoint. It is best you consult with a tax adviser and/or attorney before making any final decisions.

Check out another book by Greg Shields

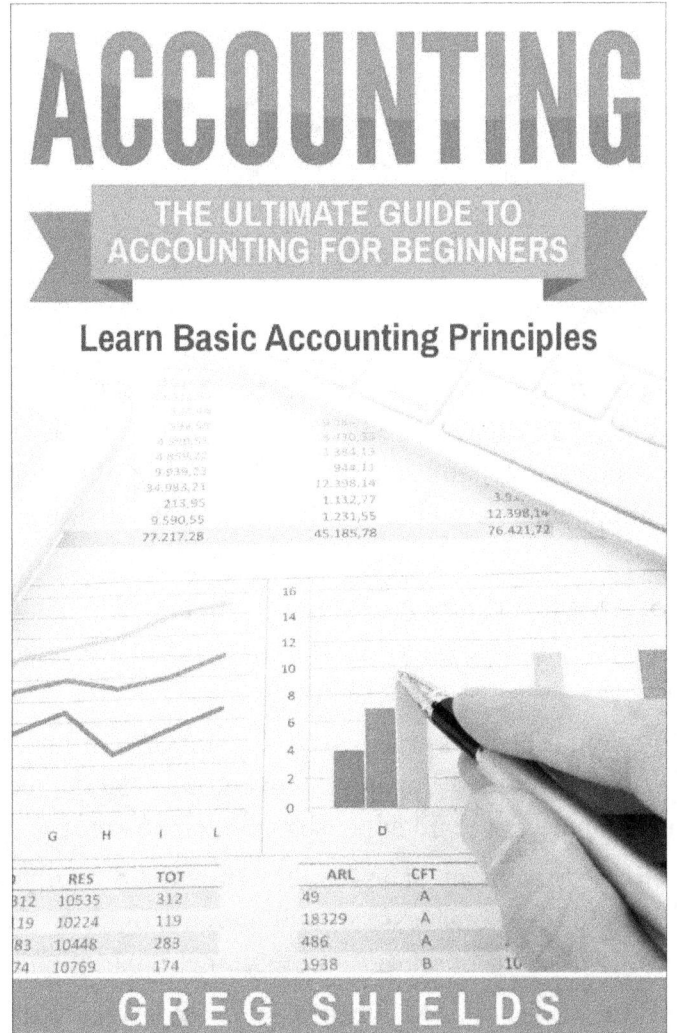

Glossary

Accrual accounting- More complex system of accounting where it allows to extend customers credit and in which one records sales or purchases immediately, and also allows for timing of cash payments, such as prepayments, which allows more accurate financial statements

Articles of Organization- A document filed with a state or local agency establishing an LLC and containing basic information about the business

Asset- Anything a business can use as capital or turn into cash, this includes actual cash, business inventory, land, equipment, intellectual property, prepaid expenses, or accounts receivable

Balance sheet- Statement of assets, liabilities and equity and their distribution within a business at any given point in time. The equation being assets = liabilities + equity or any variation thereof

Capital Gain- Gain realized when a business owner sells an asset for more than its purchase price

Cash accounting- Simplified system of accounting where cash is recorded as it changes hands, either by receiving a cash or check payment or electronically

Claim- to assert to be rightfully due

Corporation- a type of business that is recognized as a legal entity and recognized as such in law

Cost of goods sold (COGS)- The total of all goods and materials utilized in order to make product or service for sale.

Dissolution- Closing down or dismissal of business or partnership, either by the owner or state where the LLC is recognized

Double-entry accounting- System of accounting where a minimum of two accounts are affected whenever a transaction occurs

Double Taxation- income taxes paid twice from a single source of income

Employer Identification Number (EIN)- A unique number issued by the Internal Revenue Service to a business which allows it to be identified for federal tax purposes, similar to a social security number for an individual

Equity- Any capital contribution of a member or owner of a business.

Finished goods- Inventory account used in a manufacturing environment where completed goods are ready for sale

First-in, first-out (FIFO)- Inventory accounting method where the oldest items and their pricing is recorded as sold first, but does not mean the actual oldest item was sold.

Fiscal tax year- The actual one-year tax period a company elects to follow which may or may not coincide with the calendar year

Foreign LLC- Any LLC with headquarters outside of the state where the LLC is registered

Initial Public Offering (IPO)- a company's initial offering for sale of its publicly-traded stock

Internal controls- Controls utilized within a company in order to prevent fraud or embezzlement of money or assets

Last-in, first-out (LIFO)- Inventory accounting method where the latest item and price is recorded as sold first

Liability- A legal responsibility of a person or company which can be a debt, a salary payable or other obligation

Managing member- any member of an LLC who also runs the business operation

Member- any individual who owns interest in an LLC

Operating agreement- a document that outlines the rules and regulations for the management on an LLC

Ownership percentages- LLC ownership can be allocated in two ways: 1. By percentage, 2. By units of ownership. A unit of ownership is similar to a share of company stock. The difference in LLC ownership and company stock is the freedom of determining ownership percentages, even if Joe contributes $25,000 to ownership he may elect to be a silent partner, meanwhile Fred contributes no capital but has a 50% ownership because he had elected to run the day-to-day operations of the business.

Partnership- a business arrangement where two or more parties form to advance their mutual interests

Pass-Through Entity- a form of business or tax situation where profits are passed through to the business owner or members

Piercing the Corporate Veil- a situation where courts set aside an LLC or corporation's limited liability protections and holds the owner or shareholders personably liable for its debts

Profit and loss (P&L) statement- A statement showing the performance of a business for a specified period of time accounting for any income taken in, cost of goods sold, and expenses paid out. A positive result after all these factors are accounted for is a profit, a negative result is considered a loss.

Registered agent- a designated person who elects to receive legal notices on behalf of an LLC

"S" Corporation- a corporation that elects to pass its income or losses directly on to its shareholders for federal tax purposes

Share- a portion of the equal parts in which a company's capital is divided

Shareholder- owner of shares of a company

Single-entry accounting- Accounting system where only one account is used to record multiple transactions similar to how a checkbook is used to record deposits from income and expenses/bill payments

Sole proprietorship- simplest form of a business entity in which a single person is responsible for its debts and liabilities

Statement of cash flows- A statement for a specified period that focuses on cash generated and used in that timeframe

Tort- a wrongful act (not involving a contract) resulting in a lawsuit or injunction

Work in progress (WIP)- Inventory account used in a manufacturing environment where actual goods are in progress of being completed

Working Capital- Current assets, such as your accounts receivables, inventory, and cash minus current liabilities including accounts payable and debt payments due within one year. A measure of a company's immediate liquidity.

Write-off, written off- Any expense used for business purposes that can be claimed against business income for tax purposes. These expenses decrease taxable income for a business.

www.ingramcontent.com/pod-product-compliance
Lightning Source LLC
Chambersburg PA
CBHW070506220526
45467CB00002B/592